Li K

Even You Can Hack!

WINDOWS
HACKING

Even You Can Hack!

WINDOWS HACKING

Learn Windows Hacking
the Easy Way

ANKIT FADIA

VIKAS® PUBLISHING HOUSE PVT LTD

VIKAS® PUBLISHING HOUSE PVT LTD

A-22, Sector-4, **Noida** - 201301 (UP)
Phone: 0120-4078900 • Fax: 4078999
Regd. Office: 576, Masjid Road, Jangpura, **New Delhi**-110 014
E-mail: *helpline@vikaspublishing.com* • *www.vikaspublishing.com*
• First Floor, N.S. Bhawan, 4th Cross, 4th Main, Gandhi Nagar,
  Bangalore-560 009 • Phone: 080-22204639
• Damodhar Centre, New No. 62, Old No. 59, Nelson Manickam Road,
  Aminjikarai, **Chennai**-600 029 • Phone: 044-23744547, 23746090
• 35, Palm Avenue, **Kolkata**-700 019 • Phone: 033-22833494
• F-20, Nand Dham Industrial Estate, Marol,
  Andheri (East), **Mumbai**-400 059 • Phone: 022-28502333, 28502324

Distributors:

UBS PUBLISHERS' DISTRIBUTORS PVT LTD

5, Ansari Road, **New Delhi**-110 002
  • Ph. 011-23273601, 23266646 • Fax: 23276593, 23274261
• 10, First Main Road, Gandhi Nagar, **Bangalore**-560 009 • Ph. 080-22253903
• Z-18, M P Nagar, Zone-1, **Bhopal**-462 011 • Ph. 0755-4203183, 4203193
• 60, Nelson Manickam Road, Aminjikarai, **Chennai**-600 029
  • Ph. 044-23746222
• 40/7940, Convent Road, **Ernakulam**-682 035 • Ph. 0484-2353901, 2363905
• NVK Towers, 2nd Floor, Adjacent to old Hyderabad Stock Exchange,
  3-6-272 Himayat Nagar, **Hyderabad**-500 029 • Ph. 040-23262573/74
• 8/1-B, Chowringhee Lane, **Kolkata**-700 016 • Ph. 033-22521821, 22522910
• 9 Ashok Nagar, Near Pratibha Press, Gautam Buddha Marg, Latush Road,
  Lucknow-226 001 • Ph. 0522-2294134, 3014010
• 2nd Floor, Apeejay Chambers, 5 Wallace Street, Fort, **Mumbai**-400 001
  • Ph. 022-66376922-3, 66102069 • Fax: 66376921
• GF, Western Side, Annapoorna Complex, Naya Tola, **Patna**-800 004
  • Ph. 0612-2672856, 2673973
• 680 Budhwar Peth, 2nd Floor, Appa Balwant Chowk, **Pune**-411 002
  • Ph. 020-24461653, 24433976

First Edition 2006
Reprinted in 2006, 2007
Second Reprint 2008

Copyright © Ankit Fadia, 2006

Printed at Sanjay Printers, Delhi-110032

PREFACE

First introduced in 1985 as an add-on to MS –DOS, Microsoft Windows operating system is today one of the most popular and widely used platforms in the world. More than 1.15 billion computers use one of the many generations of Windows. This popularity has led Windows to be quite vulnerable, as crackers have targeted Windows for their attacks more than lesser-used operating systems.

As an operating system Windows assumes that its average user has very low computing skills and takes onto itself a lot of the 'burden' of managing the ever-more powerful and complex computers that it is loaded on. In fact, it has been observed that the MS Windows interface 'isolates' the user from a little too much of the inner workings of the computer.

Windows Hacking throws light on how to tweak the operating system to make the most of all its features, functionality, looks and feel. The comprehensively researched security tips, tricks and hacks covered in this book shall allow readers to secure Windows better, customize almost all its aspects to suit personal preferences and make it work the extra mile. After reading this book, not only will readers be able to protect their Windows system against the most common vulnerabilities, loopholes and threats, but will also be able to play cool tricks to impress their friends. A fun and light read that will also make the reader more aware of Windows related security issues and practices.

Want to improve the security of your Windows system? Want to customize the look and feel of your Windows system? Want to control all aspects and features of your Windows System? Want to play harmless pranks on your friends and trick them? *Windows Hacking* will ensure that even you can hack!

Ankit Fadia

fadia.ankit@gmail.com
www.hackingmobilephones.com

CONTENTS

Chapter 1

PASSWORDS

Introduction

Passwords are one of the oldest forms of authentication mechanism being used on systems across the world. Password prompts, where one is asked to enter the correct username-password pair, are what prevent infiltration and ensure privacy. Every computer criminal aspires to be able to go past the password prompt and gain illegal access to sensitive data for malicious purposes. Even the data on Windows systems is protected through the password protection mechanism.

As soon as one boots a Windows system, one is greeted by a welcome password prompt, which on most systems can, unfortunately, be bypassed simply by clicking on the *Cancel* button. Even after the Windows session has begun, it is possible for a user to enforce password protection on specific files, folders or drives. In other words, passwords have also become one of the most commonly used authentication mechanisms on systems worldwide. It would be safe to say that passwords are the most important security mechanisms ever deployed.

Unfortunately, most people continue to treat passwords as a set of random and useless characters. It is also becoming increasingly easy for computer criminals to break password protection mechanisms using sophisticated tools and algorithms. Moreover, the most common passwords continue to remain a *blank* or same as the username. Once an attacker finds out the victim's password there are endless number of malicious activities that can be carried out. Hence, it has become very important for Windows users to take basic precautions to improve the overall security of the system. In this section we discuss some of the most common tips and tricks related to passwords and authentication that every Windows user must know.

> **Warning:** Although all examples explained in this section have been thoroughly tested on various platforms, it is always a good idea to back up all system files involved to avoid any accidental damage.

Protecting User Privacy at Logon Prompts

(For all Windows versions)

Prank Quotient: Low   *Security Quotient:* High

Normally, at the time of logging into a Windows system, it is possible to find out information on the last user since his/her details are stored in the cache memory. It is always a good security and privacy practice to prevent this information from being displayed by executing the following registry tweak:

1. Open the *regedit.exe* file.

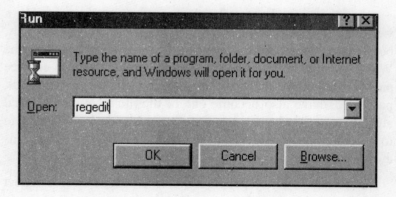

2. Search for, or create, the following registry key:

   For Windows 2000 or XP:

   HKEY_LOCAL_MACHINE\SOFTWARE\Microsoft\ Windows\CurrentVersion\Policies\System

For Windows 95, 98 or Windows ME:

HKEY_LOCAL_MACHINE\Network\Logon

For Windows NT:

*HKEY_LOCAL_MACHINE\SOFTWARE\Microsoft\
WindowsNT\CurrentVersion\Winlogon*

3. Create a new WORD value (within the above registry key) called *Dont* *splayLastUserName* and set its value to 1 to prevent the last username from displaying, and to 0 to implement the default settings.

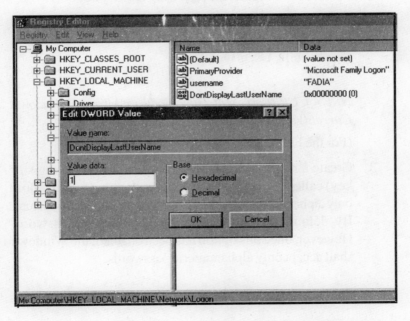

4. Exit the Windows registry and restart the Windows session for the change to be applied.

It is also possible to implement the above by simply creating and executing a .reg extension file containing the data below:

REGEDIT4
[Registry Key depending upon Windows version]
"DontDisplayLastUserName"="1"

Improving Password Security Settings

(For all Windows versions)

Prank Quotient: Low   *Security Quotient:* High

The biggest security loophole plaguing systems across the world is the tendency of users to choose a poor password. Hence, a number of system administrators prefer to force users to use a strong password through a small but effective registry tweak:

1. Open the *regedit.exe* file.

2. Search for, or create, the following registry key:

    HKEY_CURRENT_USER\Software\Microsoft\Windows\ CurrentVersion\Policies\Network

    (For Specific Users Only)

    OR

    HKEY_CURRENT_MACHINE\Software\Microsoft\Windows\ CurrentVersion\Policies\Network

    (For the Entire Machine)

3. Create a new DWORD value (within the above registry key) called *AlphanumPwds* and set its value to 1, to allow only alphanumeric passwords and to 0 to disable this feature. By default, Windows accepts any kind of password. However, once this option has been enabled, the Windows shall accept only alphanumeric passwords.

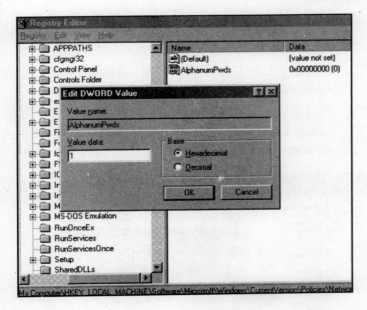

4. Exit the Windows registry and restart the Windows session for the change to be applied.

It is also possible to implement the above by simply creating and executing a .reg extension file containing the data given below:

REGEDIT4

[HKEY_CURRENT_USER\Software\Microsoft\Windows
CurrentVersion\Policies\Network]

"AlphanumPwds"="1"

Configuring a Minimum Windows Logon Password Length

(For all Windows versions)
Prank Quotient: Low   *Security Quotient:* High

Another strategy that system administrators often use to improve security is to configure a minimum required password length setting for all users. This can be done with the help of the following registry tweak:

1. Open the *regedit.exe* file.

2. Search for, or create, the following registry key:

   HKEY_CURRENT_USER\Software\Microsoft\Windows\ CurrentVersion\Policies\Network

3. Create a new binary value (within the above registry key) called *MinPwdLen* and set its data value to the minimum number of required characters that every password must have.

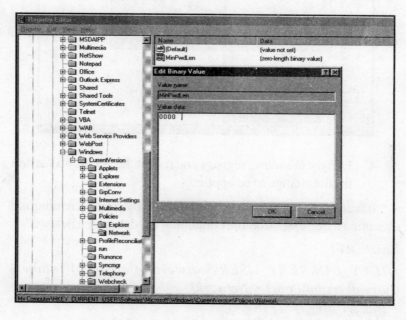

4. Exit the Windows registry and restart the Windows session for the change to be applied.

It is also possible to implement the above by simply creating and executing a .reg extension file containing the data below:

REGEDIT4

[HKEY_CURRENT_USER\Software\Microsoft\Windows\ CurrentVersion\Policies\Network]

"MinPwdLen"= "Enter Length here"

Choosing a Strong Password

(For all Windows versions)
Prank Quotient: Low   *Security Quotient:* High

Please refer to Checklists section later in this book for more information on this topic.

Preventing Windows Logon Password Caching

(For all Windows versions)
Prank Quotient: Low   *Security Quotient:* High

Another security risk that most Windows systems pose is that a copy of the user's password is stored on the local system. This further opens up the system to malicious attacks. However, system

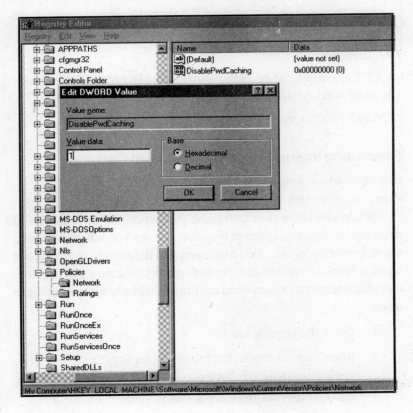

administrators can easily prevent password caching by simply following the steps below:

1. Open the *regedit.exe* file.

2. Search for, or create, the following registry key:

    HKEY_LOCAL_MACHINE\Software\Microsoft\Windows\ CurrentVersion\Policies\Network

3. Create a new DWORD value (within the above registry key) called *DisablePwdCaching* and set its value to 1 to prevent password caching and to 0 to enable it.

4. Exit the Windows registry and restart the Windows session for the change to be applied.

It is also possible to implement the above by simply creating and executing a .reg extension file containing the data given below:

REGEDIT4

[HKEY_LOCAL_MACHINE\Software\Microsoft\Windows\ CurrentVersion\Policies\Network]

"DisablePwdCaching"="1"

Preventing Internet Explorer Password Caching

(For all Windows versions)

Prank Quotient: Low   *Security Quotient:* High

When you enter your username-password pair on a password protected website on Internet Explorer, it asks you whether to save the information or not. This also opens up the system to malicious attacks, privacy invasion and criminal activity. System administrators can also prevent this password caching by simply following these steps:

1. Open the *regedit.exe* file.

2. Search for, or create, the following registry key:

    HKEY_CURRENT_USER\Software\Microsoft\Windows\ CurrentVersion\Internet Settings

3. Create a new DWORD value (within the above registry key) called *DisablePasswordCaching* and set its value to 1 to prevent password caching, and to 0 to enable it.

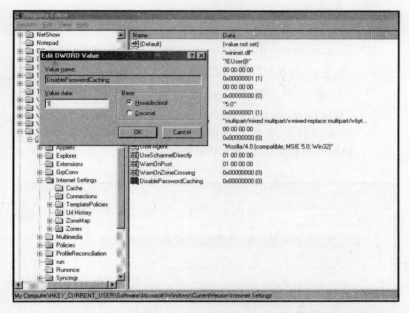

4. Exit the Windows registry and restart the Windows session for the change to be applied.

It is also possible to implement the above by simply creating and executing a .reg extension file containing the following data:

REGEDIT4

[HKEY_CURRENT_USER\Software\Microsoft\Windows\CurrentVersion\Internet Settings]

"DisablePasswordCaching"="1"

Customizing the Password Prompt Welcome Message

(For Windows 2000, XP and NT)
Prank Quotient: Medium   *Security Quotient:* Medium

Taking the previous registry tweak to a higher level, it is actually possible to customize the welcome message displayed on the password prompt dialog box. This can be done by simply following the steps below:

1. Open the *regedit.exe* file.

2. Search for the following registry key or create a new one:

    HKEY_LOCAL_MACHINE\SOFTWARE\Microsoft\ WindowsNT\CurrentVersion\Winlogon

3. Create a new string entry called *LogonPrompt* and change its data value to the customized message text that you want to be displayed at the logon prompt.

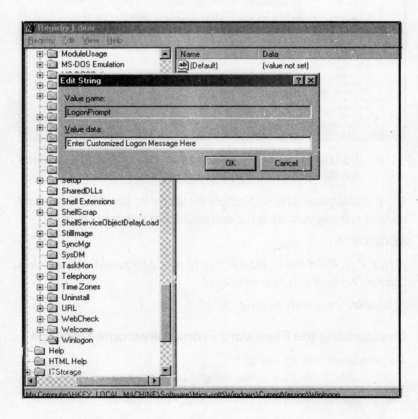

4. Exit the Windows registry and restart the Windows session for the change to be applied.

It is also possible to implement the above by simply creating and executing a .reg extension file containing the undermentioned data:

REGEDIT4

[HKEY_LOCAL_MACHINE\SOFTWARE\Microsoft\WindowsNT\ CurrentVersion\Winlogon]

"LogonPrompt"= "Enter Message Here"

Customizing the Password Prompt Title

(For Windows 2000, NT and XP)

Prank Quotient: Medium   *Security Quotient:* Medium

The Windows password prompt dialog box title can also be changed by simply following the undermentioned messages:

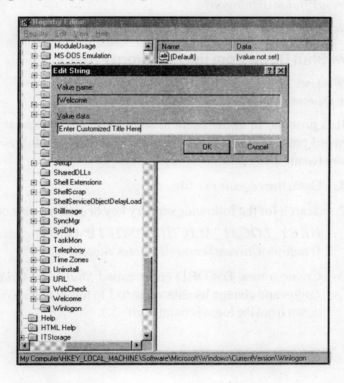

1. Open the *regedit.exe* file.

2. Search for the following registry key or create a new one:

    HKEY_LOCAL_MACHINE\SOFTWARE\Microsoft\ WindowsNT\CurrentVersion\Winlogon

3. Create a new string entry called *Welcome* and change its data value to the customized title that you want to be displayed at the logon prompt dialog box.

4. Exit the Windows registry and restart the Windows session for the change to be applied.

It is also possible to implement the above by simply creating and executing a.reg extension file containing the following data:

REGEDIT4

[HKEY_LOCAL_MACHINE\SOFTWARE\Microsoft\WindowsNT \CurrentVersion\Winlogon]

"Welcome"= "Enter Title Here"

Allow Shut Down from the Password Prompt

(For Windows 2000, NT and XP)

Prank Quotient: Low   *Security Quotient:* Medium

It is possible to allow users to shut down the system at the password prompt dialog box by simply executing the following registry tweak:

1. Open the *regedit.exe* file.

2. Search for the following registry key or create a new one:

    HKEY_LOCAL_MACHINE\SOFTWARE\Microsoft\ Windows\CurrentVersion\Policies\System

3. Create a new DWORD entry called *Shutdown Without Logon* and change its data value to 1 to allow users to shut down from the login prompt itself.

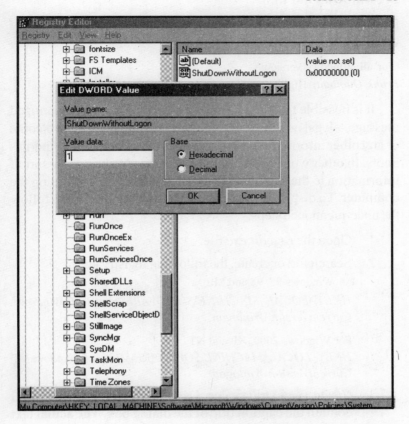

4. Exit the Windows registry and restart the Windows session for the changes to be applied. The next time you boot the system, a Shutdown button shall be displayed along with the other regular details.

It is also possible to implement the above by simply creating and executing a .reg extension file containing the data given below:

REGEDIT4

[HKEY_LOCAL_MACHINE\SOFTWARE\Microsoft\Windows\ CurrentVersion\Policies\System]

"ShutdownWithoutLogon"="1"

Displaying a Customized Banner when Windows Boots

(For all Windows versions)

Prank Quotient: High   *Security Quotient:* High

It is possible to display a dialog box containing a customized message—legal notice, privacy policy, warning, friendly welcome or any other information—before logon every time that Windows boots. In other words, this feature can be used to bring any sort of information to the user's notice before the user can start using the computer. To display such a customized banner one has to follow the undermentioned steps:

1. Open the *regedit.exe* file.

2. Search for, or create, the following registry key:

    For Windows 95, 98 and ME:

    HKEY_LOCAL_MACHINE\SOFTWARE\Microsoft\Windows\ CurrentVersion\Winlogon

    For Windows 2000, XP and NT:
    HKEY_LOCAL_MACHINE\SOFTWARE\Microsoft\WindowsNT\ CurrentVersion\Winlogon

3. Create a new string value, *LegalNoticeCaption*, which shall contain the caption title of the dialog box. The actual text for the caption title can be entered by right clicking on this string value and selecting the Modify option.

4. Create another string value, *LegalNoticeText*, which shall contain the body of the message displayed in the dialog box.

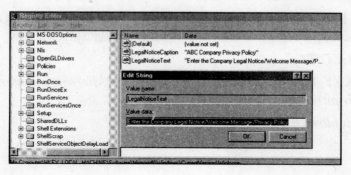

5. Exit the Windows registry. You might have to restart the Windows session for the changes to come into affect. The next time you start Windows, you shall be greeted by a message.

It is also possible to implement the above by simply creating and executing a file with a .reg extension containing the following data:

REGEDIT4

[HKEY_LOCAL_MACHINE\SOFTWARE\Microsoft\Windows\ CurrentVersion\Winlogon]

"LegalNoticeCaption"= "Caption here."

"LegalNoticeText"="Body Text here."

Requiring CTRL + ALT + Del to be Pressed Before Login

(For Windows 2000 and XP)

Prank Quotient: Low   *Security Quotient:* High

It is possible to force users to press the CTRL + ALT + DEL keys before the login authentication process begins on a Windows system. This additional security feature can be enabled by following the undermentioned steps:

1. Open the *regedit.exe* file.

2. Search for the following registry key or create a new one:

   HKEY_LOCAL_MACHINE\SOFTWARE\Microsoft\WindowsNT\ CurrentVersion\Winlogon

3. Create a new DWORD entry called *DisableCAD* and modify its data value to 0 to require CTRL + ALT + DEL keys to be pressed, and to 1 to disable this feature.

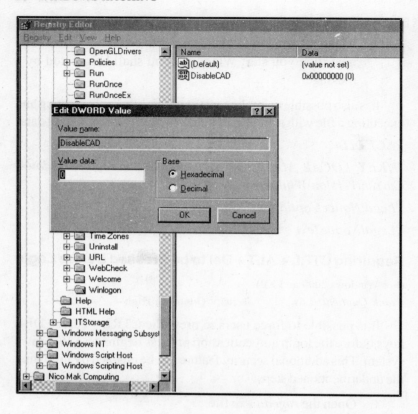

4. Exit the Windows registry and restart the Windows session for the change to be applied.

It is also possible to implement the above by simply creating and executing a .reg extension file containing the following data:

REGEDIT4

[HKEY_LOCAL_MACHINE\SOFTWARE\Microsoft\WindowsNT\ CurrentVersion\Winlogon]

"DisableCAD"="0"

Bypassing the Windows Screensaver Password—I

(For all Windows versions)

Prank Quotient: High   *Security Quotient:* High

A majority of users tend to use screensavers on their computer either to keep snoopers at bay or just because screensavers tend to look good! It is also possible for a user to password protect a screensaver. In other words, if a screensaver has been password protected, once the screensaver appears, the correct password is required to remove it. Let us assume a scenario wherein you have forgotten your own Windows screensaver password or want to reset your friend's screensaver password for some reason, this is all you can do.

1. Open the *regedit.exe* file.

2. Search for the following registry key:

   HKEY_CURRENT_USER\Control Panel\Desktop

3. Delete the *ScreenSave_Data* value in order to reset the screensaver password.

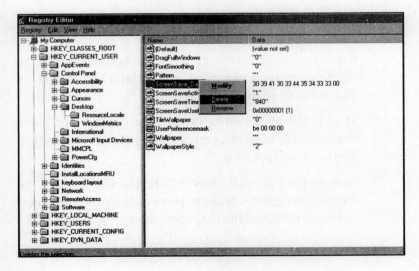

4. Exit the Windows registry. You might need to restart the Windows session in order to allow the changes to take effect.

5. The next time a password protected screensaver runs on the target computer, irrespective of what password is entered at the prompt, your password shall be accepted.

Bypassing the Windows Screensaver Password–II

(For all Windows versions)

Prank Quotient: High   *Security Quotient:* High

Yet another method by which the Windows screensaver password can be bypassed is as follows:

1. Locate the screensaver file that is normally located in the system directory. For example, *3dpipe~1.scr*

2. Open the above screensaver file in the MS DOS editor:

   c:\>cd winnt

   c:\winnt>cd system32

   c:\winnt\system32>edit /70 3dpipe~1.scr

3. Search for the following string:

   VerifyScreenSavePwd

   It is this keyword that directs the operating system to prompt for the screensaver password, without which the user is not allowed to do anything on the system.

4. Modify the above string by simply changing any one character. For example, you can change the above string to *VerifyScreenSavePwd*.

5. Save the file and exit the MS DOS Editor. The next time the screensaver becomes active no password prompt is displayed since you modified the *VerifyScreenSavePwd* keyword.

Disabling the Windows Screensaver

(For all Windows versions)

Prank Quotient: High   *Security Quotient:* High

It is possible to completely disable the Windows screensaver from running by simply following the undermentioned steps:

1. Open the *regedit.exe* file.

2. Search for the following registry key:

    HKEY_CURRENT_USER\Software\Policies\Microsoft\Windows\ControlPanel\Desktop

3. Within the above registry key, create a new DWORD value named *ScreenSaveActive* and set its value to 0 to block the screensaver.

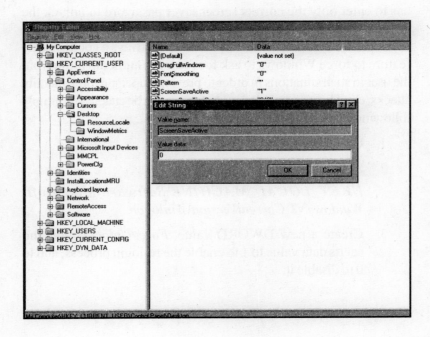

4. Exit the Windows registry. You might need to restart the Windows session in order to allow the changes to take effect.

It is also possible to implement the above by simply creating and executing a file with a .reg extension containing the following data:

REGEDIT4

[HKEY_CURRENT_USER\Software\Policies\Microsoft\Windows\ Control Panel\Desktop]

"ScreenSaveActive"="0"

Forcing Re-login at the Screensaver Password Prompt

(For Windows 2000, NT and XP)

Prank Quotient: Low   *Security Quotient:* High

Each time a password protected Windows screensaver runs one has to enter only the correct screensaver password to unlock the system. In other words, the user account details are not authenticated each time the system has to be unlocked. It is always a good security feature to force Windows to ask for the login authentication from the user in such situations in order to prevent impersonation, identity attacks, etc. This additional security feature can be enabled by simply following the undermentioned steps:

1. Open the *regedit.exe* file.

2. Search for the following registry key:

   HKEY_LOCAL_MACHINE\Software\Microsoft\ WindowsNT\CurrentVersion\Winlogon

3. Create a new DWORD value, *ForceUnlockLogon* and set its data value to 1 to enable the re-login process, and to 0 to disable it.

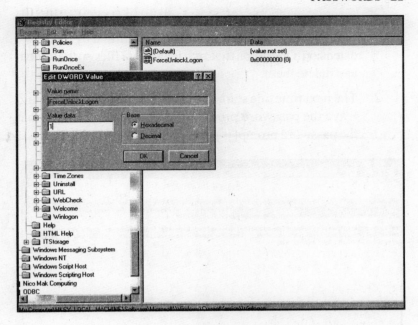

4. Exit the Windows registry. You might have to restart the Windows session for the changes to come into effect.

It is also possible to implement the above by simply creating and executing a file with a .reg extension containing the data below:

REGEDIT4

[HKEY_LOCAL_MACHINE\Network\Logon]

"ForceUnlockLogon"="1"

Disabling the Password Prompt during Logon

(For all Windows 9x editions)

Prank Quotient: Medium   *Security Quotient:* Low

Each time one boots a Windows system, the password prompt dialog box greets the user asking for the correct username-password pair. Sometimes, this can get extremely irritating and one wishes to do away with it. It is indeed possible to prevent this dialog box from showing up each time by simply following the steps below:

1. On Windows systems, the logon password information is stored in password list files that are identified by their .pwl extension. One needs to search for all .pwl files on the system and delete them.

2. The next time one starts the Windows session, one should leave the password prompt box empty. This ensures that the password prompt is never displayed again.

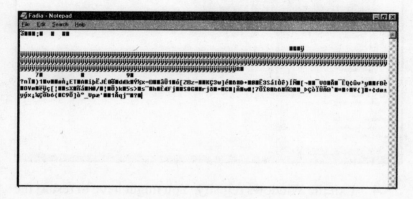

Disabling the Cancel Button in the Password Prompt

(For Windows 95, 98 and Me)

Prank Quotient: Low   *Security Quotient:* High

Almost all Windows systems have an option of enabling multiple users on the same system and using the username-password pair to authenticate the identity of specific users. Unfortunately, on older versions of Windows, a user can easily bypass the logon password prompt by simply clicking on the *Cancel* button. Hence, many system administrators have started forcing users to logon by implementing a small registry tweak:

1. Open the *regedit.exe* file.

2. Search for the following registry key:

   *HKEY_USERS\DEFAULT\Software\Microsoft\Windows\\
   CurrentVersion\Run*

3.   Create a new string entry named *NoLogon* and set its data value to:

   RUNDLL32 shell32,SHExitWindowsEx 0

5.   Exit the windows registry. You might have to restart the Windows session for the changes to come into effect. The next time you start your system, pressing the *Cancel* button at the password prompt shall not allow you to bypass the logon authentication process.

It is also possible to implement the above by simply creating and executing a file with a .reg extension containing the undermentioned data:

REGEDIT4

[HKEY_USERS\DEFAULT\Software\Microsoft\Windows \CurrentVersion\Run]

"NoLogon"= "RUNDLL32 shell32,SHExitWindowsEx 0"

Disabling the Change Password Option

(For Windows 2000, Me, XP and NT)
Prank Quotient: Low   *Security Quotient:* High

It is possible to disable the *Change Password* option on the security page by simply executing the following registry tweak:

1.   Open the *regedit.exe* file.

2.   Search for the following registry key:

   HKEY_LOCAL_MACHINE\Software\Microsoft\Windows\ CurrentVersion\Policies\System

3.   Create a new DWORD entry named *Disable Change Password* and set its data value to 0 to disable the change password option, and to 1 to enable it again.

4.   Similarly, it is also possible to create another DWORD entry named *DisableLockWorkstation* that can be used to prevent users from locking machines accidentally or intentionally.

5. Exit the Windows registry. You might have to restart the Windows session for the changes to come into effect.

It is also possible to implement the above by simply creating and executing a file with a .reg extension containing the undermentioned data:

REGEDIT4

[HKEY_LOCAL_MACHINE\Software\Microsoft\Windows\ CurrentVersion\Policies\System]

"DisableChangePassword"="1"

"DisableLockWorkstation"="1"

Cracking All Windows Passwords

(For all Windows versions)
Prank Quotient: High   *Security Quotient:* High

People nowadays not only use passwords to secure the logon option in Windows, but have also started securing various application files using inbuilt password protection mechanisms. Unfortunately, such application password security features are far from being secure and can easily be broken with the help of ready-to-use tools available on the Internet. Some of the most common Windows applications and their respective password cracking tools have been listed in the table given here.

Windows Application	Password Cracker
Zip Files	Advanced ZIP Password Recovery
All Instant Messengers	Advanced Instant Messenger Password Recovery
Windows Login Passwords	L0phtcrack
E-mail Clients like Outlook Express, Eudora Pro, etc.	Advanced Mailbox Password Recovery
Adobe Acrobat PDF Files	Advanced PDF Password Recovery
Microsoft Office Passwords	Office Key

(Contd.)

Windows Application	Password Cracker
All Windows Passwords	Advanced Windows Password Recovery
Internet Explorer Passwords	Internet Explorer Password Recovery
File Maker Pro Passwords	File Maker Key
Web Passwords	WebBrute

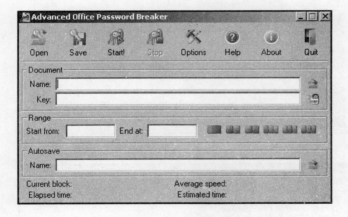

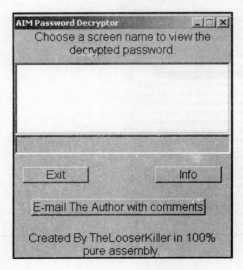

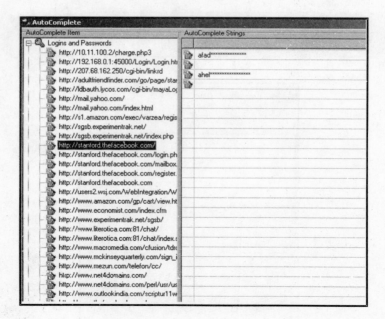

Chapter 2

THE LOOK AND FEEL

Introduction

There are millions of systems across the world running the Windows operating system. Unfortunately, the look and feel of Windows is extremely mundane, plain and boring. It usually displays the same familiar splash screen on start up, has a start button on the left bottom corner and a clock on the right corner of the screen, pops up the same context menu items when the user clicks on a certain part of the screen and so on. The bottomline is that the Windows operating system remains a very ordinary looking operating system. Moreover, Microsoft continues to give the enigmatic impression that it is not possible to play around with the Windows look and feel.

But users are smarter. They have already started using third party applications that allow them to change the look of the Windows operating system. But, why spend money on third party applications that may or may not be so effective as you would like them to be. In this section we learn a variety of interesting tweaks, tricks and tips using which it is possible to completely customize the way Windows looks, functions and feels to suit your individual personal needs and preferences.

> **Warning:** Although all examples explained here have been thoroughly tested on various platforms, it is always good to backup all system files to avoid any accidental damage.

Customizing the Startup and Shutdown Screens

(For all editions of Windows 9x)

Prank Quotient: High   *Security Quotient*: Low

The default Windows Startup and Shutdown screens can sometimes get very mundane and boring. As said earlier, they can be modified to look better. The steps are:

1. Create backups of the *Logos.sys* (The Exit screen image file is normally found in the c:\windows directory) *and Logo.sys* (The Startup screen image file is normally found in the c:\ directory) files.

2. Rename the extensions of the *Logos.sys* and *Logo.sys* files to .bmp.

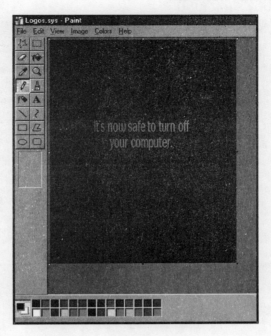

3. Now you can edit these files using graphic editors to suit your personal preferences.

4. Finally, rename these new modified files back to their original filenames and replace the older files.

5. Next time you start your Windows session you shall find that both the startup and shutdown screens have been replaced with your personally customized images.

Blocking Windows Hotkeys

(For all Windows versions)

Prank Quotient: Medium   *Security Quotient:* Medium

It is possible to prevent users from using the Windows shortcut hotkeys—like ALT + TAB and others—by simply following the steps given below:

1. Open the *regedit.exe* file.

2. Scroll down to or create the following registry key:

   HKEY_LOCAL_MACHINE\ Software\Microsoft\Windows\ CurrentVersion\Policies\ Explorer

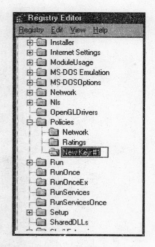

3. Create a new DWORD value named *NoWinKeys* within the above registry key and set its data value to 1 to disable the Windows hotkeys, and to 0 to enable them.

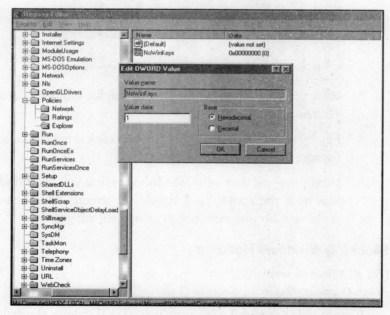

4. Exit the Windows registry and restart the Windows session for the change to be applied.

It is also possible to implement the above by simply creating and executing a .reg extension file containing the data given below:

REGEDIT4

[HKEY_LOCAL_MACHINE\Software\Microsoft\Windows\CurrentVersion\Policies\Explorer]

"NoWinKeys"="1"

Disabling Right Click on the Desktop

(For all Windows versions)
Prank Quotient: High   *Security Quotient:* High

Right clicking anywhere on the desktop pops up a number of contextual menu items like Paste, Copy, Properties and others on the screen.

It is possible to disable the user's ability to right click on the desktop by simply following the steps given under:

1. Open the *regedit.exe* file.

2. Scroll down to or create the following registry key:

   HKEY_LOCAL_MACHINE\Software\Microsoft\Windows
   CurrentVersion\Policies\Explorer

Create a new DWORD value named *NoViewContextMenu* within the above registry key and set its data value to 0 to disable the right click context menu on the desktop, and to 1 to enable it.

4. Exit the Windows registry and restart the Windows session for the change to be applied.

It is also possible to implement the above by simply creating and executing a .reg extension file containing the undermentioned data:

REGEDIT4

[HKEY_LOCAL_MACHINE\Software\Microsoft\Windows
CurrentVersion\Policies\Explorer]

"NoViewContextMenu"="0"

Disabling Right Click on the Start Button

(For all Windows versions)

Prank Quotient: High   *Security Quotient:* High

Right clicking on the Start button pops up a number of menu items like *Open, Explore, Search* and a few others on the screen.

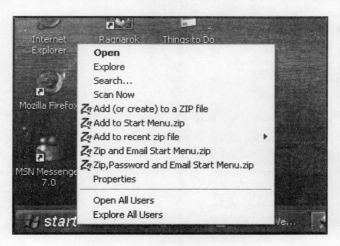

It is possible to stop these menu items from coming up by simply implementing the following registry tweak:

1. Open the *regedit.exe* file.

2. Search for the following registry key:

    HKEY_CLASSES_ROOT\Directory\Shell

    Rename the above key from shell to shell.old

3. Now search for the following registry key:

    HKEY_CLASSES_ROOT\Folder\Shell

    Rename the above key from shell to shell.old

4. Exit the Windows registry and restart the Windows session for the change to be applied.

Customize the Start Button Right Click Context Menu

(For all Windows versions)

Prank Quotient: Medium   *Security Quotient:* Low

In the last example we learnt how one can prevent users from right clicking on the Start button. It is even possible to customize the right click context menu and add new options or links to applications to it. Follow the registry tweak below:

1. Open the *regedit.exe* file.

2. Search for the registry key:

    HKEY_CLASSES_ROOT\Directory\Shell

3. Within this key, create a new sub key having the name of the application that you wish to add to the Start button, right click on context menu. This is also the text that gets displayed on the context menu when the right click is made on the Start button. For example, if you wish to add *Notepad* to the menu, the new sub key should be named Notepad.

4. Now within this newly created sub key, create yet another sub key named *Command*. In the right pane, a new string entry shall automatically appear.

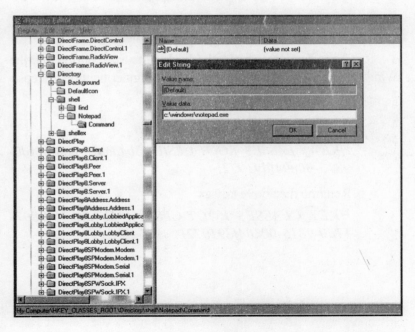

5. Change the data value of this new string entry in the right pane of the registry to point to the full pathname of the application that you want to add to the context menu. For

example, in this case since we want to add *Notepad* to the context menu, the data value of the string entry should point to the path of the Notepad Application file.

6. Exit the Windows registry. You might need to restart your Windows session for the changes to be implemented. The next time you right click on the Start button, a new menu item named *Notepad* shall also appear in the context menu.

It is also possible to remove items from this right click context menu by simply deleting the appropriate registry sub keys from the following registry key:

HKEY_CLASSES_ROOT\Directory\Shell

Disabling the Start Button and the Windows Menu Bar

(For all Windows versions)

Prank Quotient: High   *Security Quotient*: High

It is quite easy to completely disable the Start button and the Windows menu bar by simply following the undermentioned steps:

1. Open the *regedit.exe* file.

2. Search for the following registry key:

   HKEY_CLASSES_ROOT\CLSID\{5b4dae26-b807-11d0-9815-00c04fd91972}

   Rename the above key as

   *HKEY_CLASSES_ROOT\CLSID\{*5b4dae26-b807-11d0-9815-00c04fd91972}*

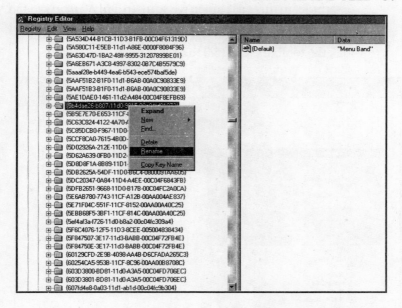

4. Exit the Windows registry and restart the Windows session for the change to be applied. You will now find that neither the Start button nor the Standard menu bars are displayed.

Locking the Toolbars

(For all Windows versions)

Prank Quotient: Low   *Security Quotient:* Medium

Usually on a Windows system, it is possible for users to customize, disable or enable various toolbars by simply clicking on the View → Toolbars option. However, it is actually possible for system administrators to lock the toolbars and prevent users from playing around with the various options. This can be carried out by simply following the steps below:

1. Open the *regedit.exe* file.

2. Scroll down to or create the following registry key:

   HKEY_LOCAL_MACHINE\Software\Microsoft\Windows\ CurrentVersion\Policies\Explorer

3. Create a new DWORD value named *NoBandCustomize* within the above registry key and set its data value to 1 to lock the toolbars, and to 0 to enable them back again.

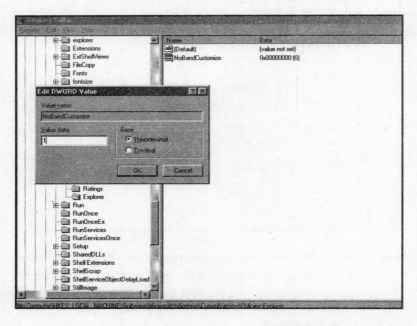

4. Exit the Windows registry and restart the Windows session for the change to be applied.

It is also possible to implement the above by simply creating and executing a .reg extension file containing the data below:

REGEDIT4

[HKEY_LOCAL_MACHINE\Software\Microsoft\Windows\ CurrentVersion\Policies\Explorer]

"NoBandCustomize"="1"

Disabling the New Menu Item

(For all Windows versions)

Prank Quotient: High   *Security Quotient:* High

Right clicking anywhere on the desktop or a folder, the New menu item gets displayed allowing users to create new objects, shortcuts etc. It is actually possible to disable this option by simply implementing the following Windows registry tweak:

1. Open the *regedit.exe* file.

2. Search for the following registry key:

    HKEY_CLASSES_ROOT\CLSID\{D969A300-E7FF-11d0-A93B-00A0C90F2719}

    Rename the above key as:

    *HKEY_CLASSES_ROOT\CLSID\{*D969A300-E7FF-11d0-A93B-00A0C90F2719}*

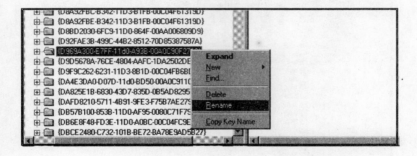

3. Exit the Windows registry and restart the Windows session for the change to be applied.

Preventing Users from Shutting Down

(For all Windows versions)

Prank Quotient: High   *Security Quotient:* High

It is actually possible for a system administrator to prevent users from using the *Shut Down* option normally accessibly through the Start menu. This hidden feature available on all Windows platforms can sometimes be invaluable for system administrators who want to restrict misuse of computers placed in airport lounges, offices, libraries and other public locations. Pranksters who want to play classic pranks on their friends also can exploit this simple registry tweak. In order to disable the *Shut Down* option, all that one needs to do is follow the steps below:

1. Open the *regedit.exe* file usually found in the windows root directory.

2. Scroll down to the following registry key:

   HKEY_CURRENT_USER\Software\Microsoft\Windows\ CurrentVersion\Policies\ Explorer

4. In the right pane, look for an existing DWORD value called *NoClose* or simply create a new one by clicking on Edit > New > DWORD Value.

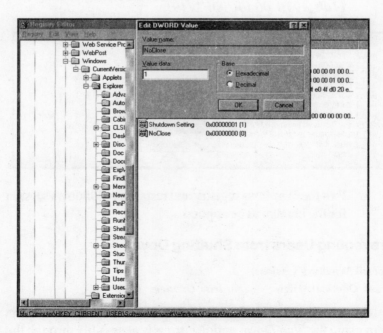

5. Set its *Data Value* field to 1 to disable the Shut down option, and to 0 to enable it.

6. Exit the Windows registry. You might need to restart the Windows session to allow for the changes to be implemented.

It is also possible to implement the above by simply creating and executing a file with a .reg extension containing the below data:

REGEDIT4

[HKEY_CURRENT_USER\Software\Microsoft\Windows\ CurrentVersion\Policies\Explorer]

"NoClose"="1"

Preventing Users from Logging Off

(For Windows 2000/ME/XP)

Prank Quotient: High   *Security Quotient:* High

Taking the previous example a step further, it is also possible to prevent users from using the *Logoff* option (normally accessible through the start menu) by simply following the below steps:

1. Open the *regedit.exe* file.

2. Search for or create the following registry key:

    HKEY_LOCAL_MACHINE\Software\Microsoft\ Windows\CurrentVersion\Policies\Explorer

3. In the right pane, create a new DWORD value called *StartMenuLogoff* (by right clicking and selecting New → (Dword Value) and set its value to 0 to enable the log off option, and to 1 to disable it.

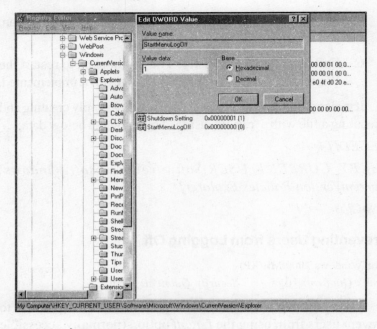

4. Exit the Windows registry and restart the Windows session for the change to be applied.

It is also possible to implement the above by simply creating and executing a .reg extension file containing the data given below:

REGEDIT4

[HKEY_LOCAL_MACHINE\Software\Microsoft\Windows\CurrentVersion\Policies\Explorer]

" StartMenuLogoff " = "1"

Forcing Logoff on the Start Menu

(For Windows 2000 and XP)

Prank Quotient: High   *Security Quotient:* Low

It is actually possible to force the *Logoff* button to appear on the Start menu by simply following the undermentioned steps:

1. Open the *regedit.exe* file.

2. Search for, or create, the following registry key:

   HKEY_CURRENT_USER\Software\Microsoft\Windows\ CurrentVersion\Policies\ Explorer

3. Create a new DWORD entry called *Force Start Menu Logoff* and set its data value to 1 to force the logoff button to appear.

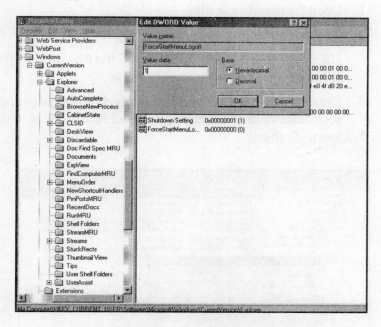

4. Exit the Windows registry and restart the Windows session for the change to be applied.

It is also possible to implement the above by simply creating and executing a .reg extension file containing the following data:

REGEDIT4

[HKEY_LOCAL_MACHINE\Software\Microsoft\Windows\ CurrentVersion\Policies\ Explorer]

"ForceStartMenuLogoff " ="1"

Allowing Quick Reboot

(For Windows 2000 and NT)
Prank Quotient: Low   *Security Quotient:* Low

It is possible to allow users to use the *quick reboot* function to start Windows again without completely shutting it down. This *quick reboot* option can be enabled with the help of the following registry tweak:

1. Open the *regedit.exe* file.

2. Search for, or create, the following registry key:

    HKEY_LOCAL_MACHINE\SOFTWARE\Microsoft\ WindowsNT\CurrentVersion\Winlogon

3. Create a new string entry called *EnableQuickReboot* and set its data value to 1 to enable the *quick reboot* option, and to 0 to disable it.

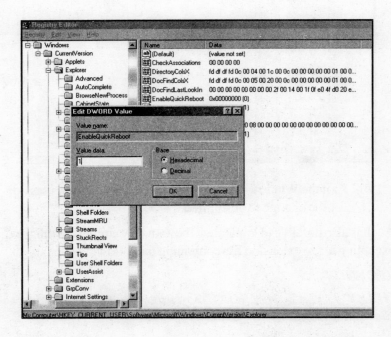

4. Exit the Windows registry and restart the Windows session for the change to be applied.

It is also possible to implement the above by creating and executing a .reg extension file containing the data:

REGEDIT4

[HKEY_LOCAL_MACHINE\SOFTWARE\Microsoft\WindowsNT\ CurrentVersion\Winlogon]

"EnableQuickReboot" = "1"

Preventing Users from using the Windows Update Option

(For all Windows versions)

Prank Quotient: High   *Security Quotient:* Medium

By default, every Windows system has a *Windows Update* option (accessible through the Start menu) that normally allows users to secure the operating system by downloading the latest patches from the Microsoft website. However, in the last few years, a number of virus infections in different parts of the world have proved that it is possible for malicious viruses to modify the default *Windows Update* website to point to a malicious website. This malicious modification is then exploited to download updated forms of the same virus!

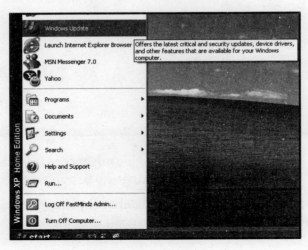

Hence, a number of system administrators have started looking for options to prevent users from using the *Windows Update* option. This tweak too is extremely easy to execute in the following steps:

1. Open the *regedit.exe* file.

2. Scroll down to or create the following registry key:

   HKEY_CURRENT_USER\Software\Microsoft\Windows\CurrentVersion\Policies\WindowsUpdate

3. Create a new DWORD value (within the above registry key) called *DisableWindowsUpdateAccess* and set its value to 1.

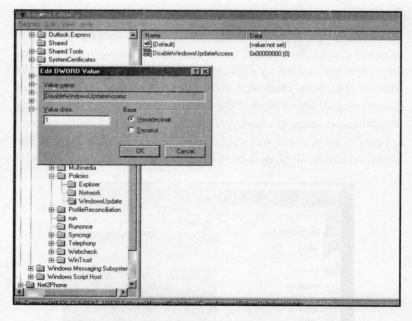

4. Exit the Windows registry. You might need to restart your Windows session for the changes to be implemented.

It is also possible to implement the above by simply creating and executing a file with a .reg extension containing the below data:

REGEDIT4

[HKEY_CURRENT_USER\Software\Microsoft\Windows\ CurrentVersion\Policies\WindowsUpdate]

"DisableWindowsUpdateAccess"="1"

Preventing Certain Applications from Running

(For Windows 2000, Me and XP)

Prank Quotient: High   *Security Quotient:* High

On many occasions it is extremely critical for a system administrator to be able to control, which applications and files can be executed and which not. There is a Windows registry tweak that allows system administrators to do exactly that—prevent specific applications and files from running. The steps that one needs to follow in order to implement such a restriction are given below:

1. Open the *regedit.exe* file.

2. Search for, or create, the following registry key:

    HKEY_CURRENT_USER\Software\Microsoft\Windows\ CurrentVersion\Policies\Explorer

3. Create a new DWORD value (within the above registry key) called *RestrictRun* (or called *DisallowRun*) and set its value to 1 to prevent applications from running, and to 0 to enable all applications to run.

4. Now search for, or create, the following new registry key:

    HKEY_CURRENT_USER\Software\Microsoft\Windows\ CurrentVersion \Policies\Explorer\RestrictRun

                                OR

    HKEY_CURRENT_USER\Software\Microsoft\Windows\ CurrentVersion \Policies\Explorer\DisallowRun

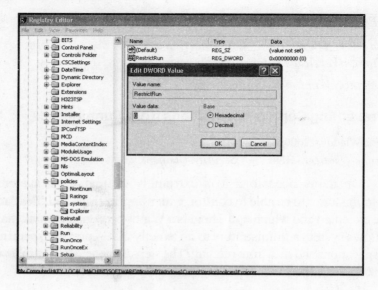

5. For each application that you want to prevent from running, create a new string entry named as consecutive numbers starting from the number 1. Set the data value of each new string entry as the filename that has to be blocked. For example, if you want to prevent Paint Brush from running, you need to set the data value of the string entry to "mspaint.exe".

6. Exit the Windows registry. You might need to restart your Windows session for the change to be implemented.

Disabling User Customization

(For all Windows versions except Windows NT)
Prank Quotient: Medium   *Security Quotient:* Medium

Some organizations may like to maintain a standard uniform look for Windows features throughout its offices. In order to ensure that users don't customize their user profiles as per personal individual tastes such organizations may prevent users from using the *user profiles* feature by the following steps:

1. Open the *regedit.exe* file.

2. Search for the following registry key:

   HKEY_LOCAL_MACHINE\Network\Logon

3. Create a new DWORD value, *UserProfiles* and set its data value to 1 to enable user profiles, and to 0 to disable them.

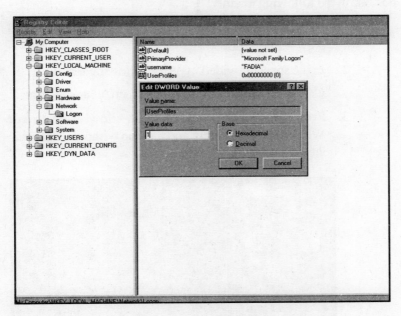

4. Exit the Windows registry. You might have to restart the Windows session for the changes to come into effect.

It is also possible to implement the above by simply creating and executing a file with a .reg extension containing the undermentioned data:

REGEDIT4

[HKEY_LOCAL_MACHINE\Network\Logon]

"UserProfiles"="0"

Exiting Windows Quickly

(For Windows 9x and 2000)
Prank Quotient: High   *Security Quotient:* Low

It is possible to create a shortcut that allows a user to immediately and quickly exit Windows through a single click on an icon. This can be done in the following manner:

1. Create a new shortcut by right clicking and selecting New > Shortcut.

2. In the space provided, type the following text in:

    C:\windows\rundll.exe user.exe,exitwindowsexec

3. Press OK. This new shortcut now allows users to exit Windows immediately and that too without displaying any warning.

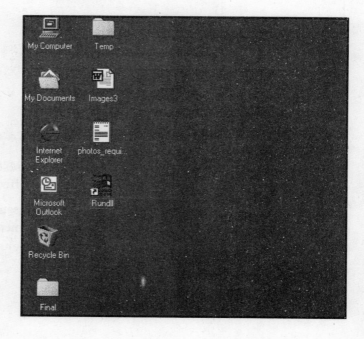

4. It is also possible to create a similar shortcut that quickly exits Windows and also restarts it. For this, the text is as below:

C:\windows\rundll.exe user.exe,exitwindows

Customizing Folder Icons

(For all Windows versions)
Prank Quotient: Medium   *Security Quotient:* Low

Unfortunately, all folders on a Windows system appear as boring yellow icons. However, it is quite easy to replace these cliché icons with snazzy looking ones by simply following the below steps:

1. Create a text file with the following contents and save it as *desktop.ini* in the folder whose icon you wish to change:

   [.ShellClassInfo]
   ICONFILE=Path of the icon

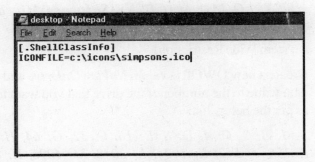

2. Similarly, it is possible to change the icon of a drive by creating a file with the following contents and saving it as *autorun.inf* in the root of the drive whose icon has to be changed:

   [Autorun]
   ICON=Path of the icon

3. It is always a good idea to change the attributes of this file to *Read Only* and *Hidden* to prevent any accidental damage.

Blocking Access to Specific Drives

(For Windows 2000, XP and ME)

Prank Quotient: Medium *Security Quotient:* High

As a useful security feature tone can block user access to specific drives. This cannot only be a good privacy protection tool but also be used as a strong intellectual property protection feature. The steps that one needs to follow in order to block access to all or specific drives are the following:

1. Open the *regedit.exe* file.

2. Search or scroll down to the following registry key:

    HKEY_LOCAL_MACHINE\Software\Microsoft\Windows\ CurrentVersion\Policies\Explorer

    (User Specific Restriction)

    OR

    HKEY_LOCAL_MACHINE\Software\Microsoft\ Windows\CurrentVersion\Policies\Explorer

    (System Wide Restriction)

3. Create a new DWORD value, *NoViewOnDrive* and set its data value to the number of the drive that you want to hide as per the below list:

    A: 1, B: 2, C: 4, D: 8, E: 16, F: 32, G: 64, H: 128, I: 256, J: 512, K: 1024, L: 2048, M: 4096, N: 8192, O: 16384, P: 32768, Q: 65536, R: 131072, S: 262144, T: 524288, U: 1048576, V: 2097152, W: 4194304, X: 8388608, Y: 16777216, Z: 33554432, ALL: 67108863

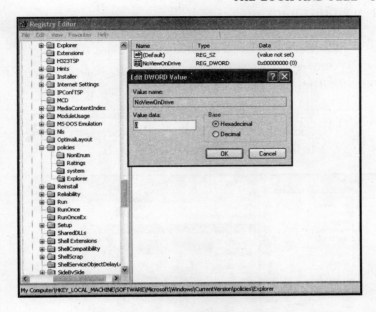

4. Exit the Windows registry. You might have to restart the Windows session for the changes to come into effect.

It is also possible to implement the above by simply creating and executing a file with a .reg extension containing the undermentioned data:

REGEDIT4

[Choose Registry Key From Key]

"NoViewOnDrive"="Drive number"

Locking the Windows Registry

(For all Windows versions)

Prank Quotient: Low *Security Quotient:* High

It is very useful for system administrators to be able to put a restriction on the editing of the Windows registry. This can be done with the help of the following simple registry tweak:

1. Open the *regedit.exe* file.

2. Search or scroll down to the following registry key:

   HKEY_CURRENT_USER\SOFTWARE\Microsoft\Windows\CurrentVersion\Policies\System

3. Create a new DWORD value, *DisableRegistryTools* and set its data value to 1 to disable registry editing, and to 0 to enable it again.

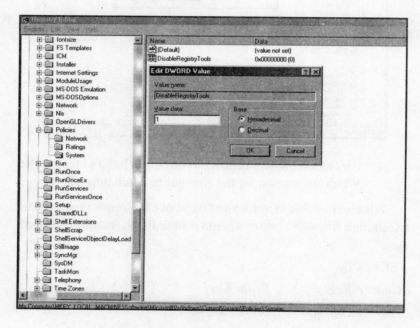

4. Exit the windows registry. You might have to restart the windows session for the changes to come into affect.

It is also possible to implement the above by simply creating and executing a file with a .reg extension containing the following data:

REGEDIT4

[HKEY_CURRENT_USER\SOFTWARE\Microsoft\Windows\CurrentVersion\Policies\System]

"DisableRegistryTools"="1"

Deleting Special Folders from the Desktop

(For all Windows versions)

Prank Quotient: High   *Security Quotient:* Medium

There are a number of special system folders—like the Recycle Bin, Printers, Network Neighborhood, Internet Explorer and many more—on all Windows desktops that simply refuse to go away! If you ever right click on any of these folders and try to delete it, you will probably be disappointed to not find the DELETE option (nor the rename, cut, copy or paste options). However, that does not mean that you cannot delete such special system folders. It is actually quite easy to delete these special system folders through the Windows registry by simply following the steps as below:

1. Open the *regedit.exe* file.

2. Search or scroll down to the following registry key:

    HKEY_LOCAL_MACHINE\Software\Microsoft\Windows\ CurrentVersion\Explorer\Desktop\Namespace

3. Each special system folder has a unique 16-byte CLSID key or the class ID that identifies an individual object that points to a corresponding key in the registry. Some of the most common system folders and their corresponding CLSID keys are as follows:

    Inbox: *{00020D76-0000-0000-C000-000000000046}*

    My Computer: *{20D04FE0-3AEA-1069-A2D8-08002B30309D}*

    Network Neighborhood: *{208D2C60-3AEA-1069-A2D7-O8002B30309D}*

    Printers: *{2227A280-3AEA-1069-A2DE-O8002B30309D}*

    Recycle Bin: *{645FF040-5081-101B-9F08-00AA002F954E}*

    Control Panel: *{21EC2020-3AEA-1069-A2DD-08002B30309D}*

    My Briefcase: *{85BBD920-42AO-1069-A2E4-08002B30309D}*

    The Microsoft Network: *{00028B00-0000-0000-C000-000000000046}*

    History: *{FF393560-C2A7-11CF-BFF4-444553540000}*

Desktop: *{00021400-0000-0000-C000-0000000000046}*

Winzip: *{E0D79300-84BE-11CE-9641-444553540000}*

Dial-Up-Networking: *{992CFFA0-F557-101A-88EC-00DD01CCC48}*

Fonts: *{BD84B380-8CA2-1069-AB1D-08000948534}*

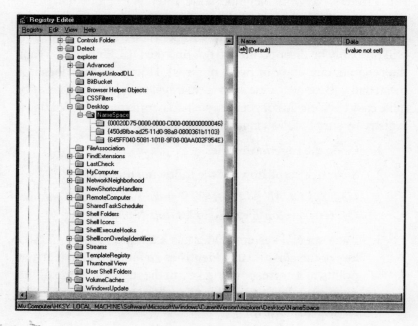

4. Each special system folder can be deleted by simply deleting its corresponding 16-byte CLSID value that can be found within the earlier mentioned key.

For example, if one wants to delete the *My Computer* icon from the desktop, one needs to just delete the following registry key:

HKEY_LOCAL_MACHINE\Software\Microsoft\Windows\ CurrentVersion\Explorer\Desktop\Namespace\{20D04FE0- 3AEA-1069-A2D8-08002B30309D}

Similarly, in order to delete the *Recycle Bin* icon from the desktop, one needs to just delete the following registry key:

HKEY_LOCAL_MACHINE\Software\Microsoft\Windows\ CurrentVersion\Explorer\Desktop\Namespace\{645FF040- 5081-101B-9F08-00AA002F954E}

5. Exit the Windows registry. You might have to restart the Windows session for the changes to come into effect.

Blocking Changes to Special Folder Locations

(For Windows 2000, XP and Me)

Prank Quotient: Low   *Security Quotient:* High

Taking the previous example a bit further, it is also possible to prevent users from changing the locations of the special folders through a registry tweak. This can be carried out with the help of a registry tweak:

1. Open the *regedit.exe* file.

2. Search or scroll down to the following registry key:

    HKEY_LOCAL_MACHINE\Software\Microsoft\Windows\ CurrentVersion\Policies\Explorer

3. Within the above registry key it is possible to create the following DWORD entries, whose value can be set to 1 to enable the restriction, and to 0 to disable it:

DWORD Value	Restriction
DisableMyPicturesDirChange	Block changes in My Pictures location.
DisableMyMusicDirChange	Block changes in My Music location.
DisableFavoritesDirChange	Block changes in My Favorites location.
DisablePersonalDirChange	Block changes in My Documents location.

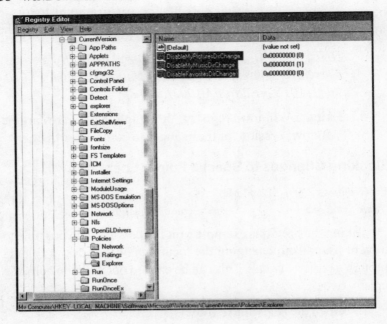

4. Exit theWindows registry. You might have to restart the Windows session for the changes to come into effect.

It is also possible to implement the above by simply creating and executing a file with a .reg extension containing the undermentioned data:

REGEDIT4

[HKEY_LOCAL_MACHINE\Software\Microsoft\Windows\ CurrentVersion\Policies\Explorer]

"DWORD Entry"="1 or 0"

Locking Floppy Drives

(For Windows 2000, XP and NT)
Prank Quotient: High   *Security Quotient:* High

By default, floppy drives are accessible to both local and remote users having the necessary privileges. This can sometimes prove to be a grave security threat. It is possible for system administrators to lock the floppy drive to prevent illicit access by implementing the following registry tweak:

1. Open the *regedit.exe* file.

2. Search for the following registry key:

   HKEY_LOCAL_MACHINE\SOFTWARE\Microsoft\ WindowsNT\CurrentVersion\Winlogon

3. Create a new string entry named *AllocateFloppies* and set its data value to 1 to ensure that only the local logged on user can access the floppy drive. On the other hand, if the string entry's data value is set to 0 then all restrictions are lifted.

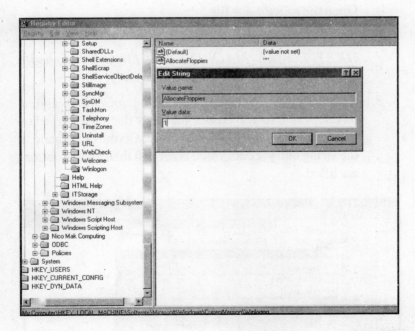

4. Exit the Windows registry. You might have to restart the Windows session for the changes to come into effect.

It is also possible to implement the above by simply creating and executing a file with a .reg extension containing the data given below:

REGEDIT4

[HKEY_LOCAL_MACHINE\SOFTWARE\Microsoft\WindowsNT\ CurrentVersion\Winlogon]

"AllocateFloppies"="1"

Locking CD-ROM Drives

(For Windows 2000, XP and NT)

Prank Quotient: High   *Security Quotient:* High

Similar to the above example, it is also possible to lock access to the CD-ROM drive by the following steps:

1. Open the *regedit.exe* file.

2. Search for the following registry key:

    HKEY_LOCAL_MACHINE\SOFTWARE\Microsoft\ WindowsNT\CurrentVersion\Winlogon

3. Create a new string entry named *AllocateCDRoms* and set its data value to 1 to ensure that only the local logged on user can access the CD-ROM drive. On the other hand, if the string entry's data value is set to 0 then all restrictions are lifted.

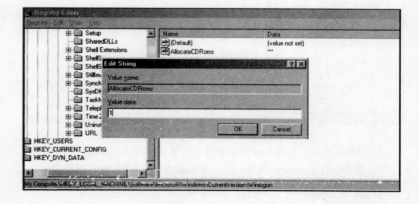

4. Exit the Windows registry. You might have to restart the Windows session for the changes to come into effect.

It is also possible to implement the above by simply creating and executing a file with a .reg extension containing the undermentioned data:

REGEDIT4

[HKEY_LOCAL_MACHINE\SOFTWARE\Microsoft\WindowsNT\ CurrentVersion\Winlogon]

"AllocateCDRoms"="1"

Adding Context Menu Items to Folders

(For all Windows versions)

Prank Quotient: High   *Security Quotient:* Low

Taking the previous section a bit further, it is also possible to add a number of items to the right click context menu of these special system folders. For example, to add items like rename, delete, cut, copy, paste and many more to all special system folders. The steps that one needs to follow in order to perform this registry tweak are:

1. Open the *regedit.exe* file.

2. Scroll down to the following registry key:

   HKEY_CLASSES_ROOT\CLSID\{CLSID Number Here}\ShellFolder

   For example, if you want to add new items to the *My Computer* context menu the following key should be opened:

   HKEY_CLASSES_ROOT\CLSID\{20D04FE0-3AEA- 1069-A2D8-08002B30309D}\ShellFolder

3. The DWORD value named *Attributes* found in the right pane of the Windows registry holds the key to adding new items to the right click context menu of the respective special system folder. The *Attributes* DWORD entry can be tweaked to add the following new menu items to system folders:

Menu Item to be Added	Modification to be made to Attributes
Rename	50 01 00 20
Delete	60 01 00 20
Rename & Delete	70 01 00 20
Copy	41 01 00 20
Cut	42 01 00 20
Copy & Cut	43 01 00 20
Paste	44 01 00 20
Copy & Paste	45 01 00 20
Cut & Paste	46 01 00 20
Cut, Copy & Paste	47 01 00 20
Default Settings	40 01 00 20

For example, in order to add the *Delete* item to the right click context menu of the Recycle Bin, simply change the data value of the *Attributes* under the corresponding registry key to 60 01 00 20.

4. Exit the Windows registry. You might have to restart the Windows session for the changes to come into effect.

It is also possible to implement the above by simply creating and executing a file with a .reg extension containing the following data:

REGEDIT4

[HKEY_CLASSES_ROOT\CLSID\{Enter CLSID Value Here}\Shell-Folder]

"Attributes"=hex:Enter Value Here

Putting Restriction on Everything in Windows

(Results vary from version to version)

Prank Quotient: High   *Security Quotient:* High

The Windows operating system tries to make it hard for users to hide or display various options, features and looks. However, it fails miserably at doing so. The Windows registry holds the key to modifying, disabling or enabling absolutely all aspects of the operating system. In other words, system administrators can place restrictions on all aspects of a user's experience using the Windows registry. Although the most common technique of putting restrictions on the user's activities is through the local registry, but sometimes certain system administrators also adopt the strategy of imposing restrictions remotely through the main server.

The easiest way to impose restrictions on a user's activities is by following the steps below:

1.   Open the *regedit.exe* file.

2.   Search for the following registry key:

     HKEY_CURRENT_USER/Software/Microsoft/ CurrentVersion/Policies/Explorer

3.   Under this registry key one can impose a number of interesting restrictions that are discussed in detail later in this section. The following new DWORD values can be created in the right pane to impose specific restrictions on the user:

     NoDeletePrinter : This DWORD value can be used to control the deletion of already installed printers. A data value of 1 means that already installed printers cannot be deleted, while a data value of 2 allows deletion of already installed printers.

     NoAddPrinter: This DWORD value is quite similar to the previous restriction feature, except that it imposes restriction on a user's ability to add new printers.

NoRun: This DWORD value can be used to either disable/hide or enable the Run option normally accessible through the start menu. A data value of 1 hides the Run option, while a data value of 0 displays it.

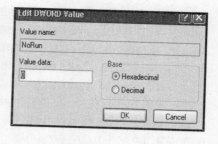

NoFind: This DWORD value can be used to either disable/hide or enable the Find option normally accessible through the start menu. A data value of 1 hides the Find option from the start menu, while a data value of 0 displays it.

NoDrives: This DWORD value can be used to hide all drives that are normally accessible through *My Computer*. A data value of 1 hides the Run option, while a data value of 0 displays it. This hidden feature of the Windows registry can be used as a very good prank to play on your unsuspecting friends! However, on a more serious note, system administrators can also use the *NoDrives* value to restrict the access privileges of a particular user.

NoNetHood: This DWORD value can be used to hide the *Network Neighborhood* icon from the desktop. A data value of 1 hides the icon, while a data value of 0 displays it.

NoInternetIcon: This DWORD value can be used to hide the *Internet Explorer* Icon from the desktop. A data value of 1 hides the icon, while a data value of 0 displays it.

NoCommonGroups: This DWORD value can be used to hide the common group folders that are normally accessible through the Start menu (Start > Programs). A data value of 1 hides the common group folders, while a data value of 0 displays them.

NoRecentDocsHistory: Each time one opens a document or a file on a Windows system, it automatically gets added to the *Recent Documents* list accessible through the Start menu. This list contains the local file access history of a computer and is quite comparable to a browser's history list. The *NoRecentDocsHistory* DWORD value can be used to prevent documents from getting added to this list. A data value of 1 removes the list from the Start menu, while a data value of 0 enables the list.

ClearRecentDocsOnExit: Taking the previous registry tweak a bit further, it is also possible to automatically clear the *Recent Documents* list each time Windows exits. The *ClearRecentDocsOnExit* DWORD value of 1 enables this feature, while a value of 0 disables it.

NoFavoritesMenu: This DWORD value can be used to either disable/hide or enable the Favorites option normally accessible through the Start menu. A data value of 1 hides the option from the start menu, while a data value of 0 displays it.

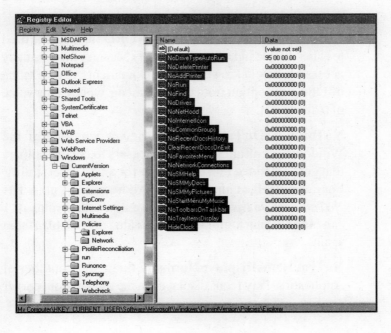

NoNetworkConnections: This DWORD value can be used to either disable/hide or enable the Network and Dial-up Connections option normally accessible through the Start menu (Start > Settings). A data value of 1 hides the option from the Start menu, while a data value of 0 displays it.

NoSMHelp: This DWORD value can be used to either disable/hide or enable the Help option normally accessible through the Start menu. A data value of 1 hides the option from the Start menu, while a data value of 0 displays it.

NoSMMyDocs: This DWORD value can be used to either disable/hide or enable the My Documents option normally accessible by clicking on Start > Documents. A data value of 1 hides the option from the Start menu, while a data value of 0 displays it.

NoSMMYPictures: This DWORD value can be used to either disable/hide or enable the My Pictures option normally accessible by clicking on Start > Documents. A data value of 1 hides the option from the Start menu, while a data value of 0 displays it.

NoStartMenuMyMusic: This DWORD value can be used to either disable/hide or enable the My Music option normally accessible by clicking on Start > Documents. A data value of 1 hides the option from the Start menu, while a data value of 0 displays it.

NoToolbarsOnTaskbar: The newer versions of the Windows operating system allow users to create toolbars that get embedded into the taskbar for quick accessibility. For example, the Quick Launch, Address, and Links. The *NoToolbarsOnTaskbar* DWORD entry with a value of 1 can hide all such toolbars, while a value of 0 enables them again.

NoTrayItemsDisplay: Normally there are a number of Application Tray Icons displayed in the right bottom corner of the screen next to the system clock. With the help of a simple registry tweak, it is possible to prevent these items from being displayed. The *NoTrayItemsDisplay* DWORD entry with a value of 1 means that the tray items shall be hidden, while a value of 0 shall display them.

HideClock: This DWORD value can be used to either disable/hide or enable the system clock normally displayed in the right bottom corner of the screen. A data value of 1 hides the clock, while a data value of 0 displays it.

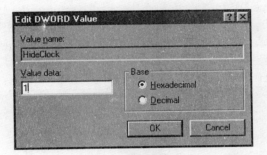

NoSetFolders: This DWORD value can be used to either remove the entire Settings folder (including all sub-folders like Control Panel, Printers, and Taskbar) normally accessible through the Start menu. A data value of 1 hides the folder, while a data value of 0 displays it.

NoSetTaskbar: It removes Taskbar system folder from the Settings option on the Start Menu. This restriction removes the Taskbar and Start Menu items from the Control Panel, and it also removes the Properties item from the Start menu context menu.

NoDesktop: This DWORD value can be used to hide the entire desktop (including all files, folders, and system folders). A data value of 1 hides the desktop and all contents on it, while a data value of 0 displays the desktop.

NoClose: It disables Shut down and prevents the user from normally shutting down Windows.

NoSaveSettings: This DWORD value can be used to either prevent your desktop settings from being changed by the user. A data value of 1 protects the desktop settings, while a data value of 0 allows the user to change the desktop settings.

DisableRegistryTools: Disable Registry Editing Tools (If you disable this option, the Windows Registry Editor (regedit.exe) too will not work.)

NoStartMenuNetworkPlaces (For Windows XP only): This DWORD value can be used to remove the *My Network Places* folder normally accessible through the Start menu. A data value of 1 hides the folder, while a data value of 0 displays it.

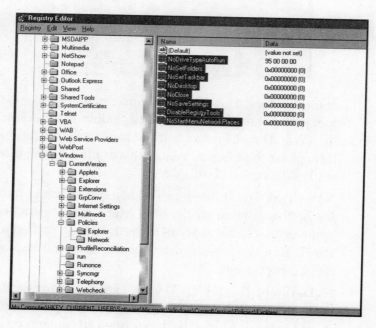

It is also possible to implement any of the above restrictions by simply creating and executing a file with a .reg extension containing the data below:

REGEDIT4

*[HKEY_CURRENT_USER\Software\Microsoft\Windows\
CurrentVersion\Policies\Explorer]*

"DWORD Entry"="VALUE"

4. Under the same key, i.e., *HKEY_CURRENT_USER/
   Software/Microsoft/Current Version/Policies* it is actually
   possible to create new sub key named *System*, within which
   the following DWORD entries can be created to get a variety
   of interesting features:

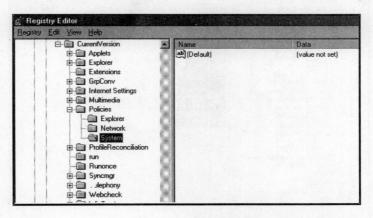

DWORD Value	Function
NoDispCPL	Hides the Control Panel.
NoDispBackgroundPage	Hides the Backgrounds Page.
NoDispScrsavPage	Hides the Screen Saver Page.
NoDispAppearancePage	Hides the Appearance Page.
NoDispSettingsPage	Hides the Settings Page.
NoSecCPL	Hides Security Page in Control Panel.
NoPwdPage	Hides Passwords Page.
NoAdminPage	Hides Remote Administration Page.

(Contd.)

DWORD Value	Function
NoProfilePage	Hides User Profiles Page.
NoDevMgrPage	Hides Device Manager Page.
NoConfigPage	Hides Hardware Profiles Page.
NoFileSysPage	Hides File System Button.
NoVirtMemPage	Hides Virtual Memory Button.

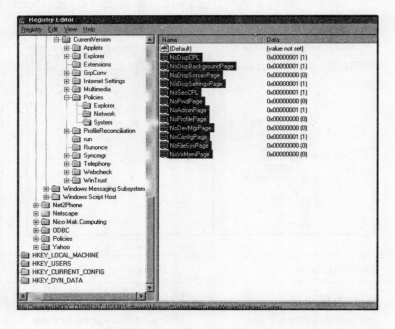

It is important to note that for each of the above DWORD entries, a data value of 1 shall enable the feature, while a value of 0 shall disable the feature. Moreover, it is possible to implement any of the above restrictions by simply creating and executing a file with a .reg extension containing the data below:

REGEDIT4

[HKEY_CURRENT_USER/Software/Microsoft/Current Version/Policies /System]

"DWORD Entry"="VALUE"

5. Under the same key, i.e., *HKEY_CURRENT_USER/ Software/Microsoft/Current Version/Policies*, it is actually possible to create yet another new sub key named *Network*. This new sub key can then be used to create a number of different DWORD entries, as mentioned below:

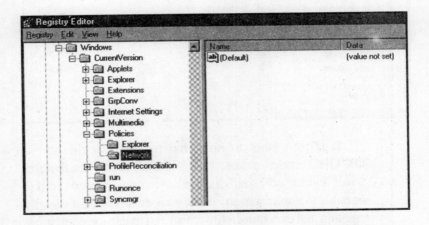

DWORD Value	Function
NoNetSetupSecurityPage	Hides the Network Security Page.
NoNetSetup	Hides the Network option in the Control Panel.
NoNetSetupIDPage	Hides the Identification Page.
NoNetSetupSecurityPage	Hides the Access Control Page.
NoFileSharingControl	Hides the File Sharing Control Page.
NoPrintSharing	Hides the Print Sharing Control Page.

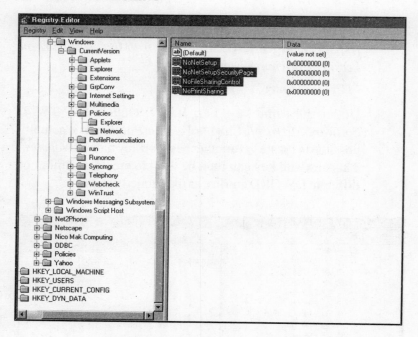

It is important to note that for each of the above DWORD entries, a data value of 1 shall enable the feature, while a value of 0 shall disable the feature. Moreover, it is possible to implement any of the above restrictions by simply creating and executing a file with a .reg extension containing the data below:

REGEDIT4

[HKEY_CURRENT_USER/Software/Microsoft/Current Version/Policies /System]

"DWORD Entry"="VALUE"

Editing Windows through Explorer.exe

(Results vary from version to version.)

Prank Quotient: High   *Security Quotient:* High

Each time one hits the CTRL + ALT + DEL keys a window titled *End Program* comes up on the screen. Invariably, amongst the application files that are shown as currently running in the memory is usually also a file called *explorer.exe*. It is this file that controls almost the entire look, feel and functioning of the Windows operating system. It is this file that holds the key to customizing Windows completely to suit one's personal preferences and likes. It is also possible to edit the *explorer.exe* file by simply following these steps:

1. It is important to remember that the *explorer.exe* file cannot be edited while the Windows operating system is still in session. Hence, the first step that one needs to follow— before one can start editing the *explorer.exe* file—is to restart the computer in the command line mode by clicking on Start > Shut Down > Restart.

2. Once you have restarted the system in the command line mode, make sure that you are in the same working directory as the *explorer.exe* file—which is normally stored in the Windows root directory.

    C:\>cd windows

3. Open the *explorer.exe* file in the MSDOS editor with the help of the */70 parameter* which basically only means that the editor window shall open with 70 columns on each line:

    C:\windows>edit /70 explorer.exe

4. The *explorer.exe* file shall now open in a blue screen containing large amounts of unrecognizable characters and a few recognizable characters as well. On most occasions, while editing the *explorer.exe* file we are more concerned with the recognizable text rather than the unrecognizable jumbled characters. For each character that is displayed in the blue screen, the corresponding Value and Line numbers are displayed on the status bar at the bottom of the screen.

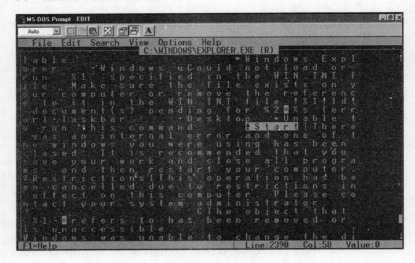

5. Scroll down and edit those parts of the *explorer.exe* file that contain recognizable text, in order to edit a variety of different aspects of the look and feel of the Windows operating system. Although editing is not too difficult, it is also handy to keep the following tips in mind:

   ✓ Ensure that the total number of characters in the *explorer.exe* file must always remain the same to avoid corruption of the operating system. Hence, one must remain very careful against accidental deletion, modification or addition while editing this file.

   ✓ The *explorer.exe* file has a number of spaces throughout its body. However, it is important to note that these spaces are different from the spaces normally created by pressing the spacebar key. The Value of the *explorer.exe* space is 0, while the value of the space created by pressing the spacebar is 32.

   ✓ Each ampersand sign (&) in the *explorer.exe* file signifies that the next character in the file shall appear underlined in the Windows operating system and is commonly used as the keyboard shortcut to execute that particular option.

✓ Normally, when you right click on the Windows desktop taskbar, a pop up context menu containing various options like *Properties, Always On Top, Auto Hide* and many others are displayed on the screen. It is possible to modify the context menu options by scrolling down to the 1300-1400 lines in the *explorer.exe* file.

✓ To edit the context menu options that appear when you right click on the Clock present in the bottom right corner of the screen, one needs to scroll down to the lines starting at 2300.

✓ To edit the Start menu options including the text that appears on the Start button one should scroll down to the lines starting at 2300.

Customizing the Look and Feel of the Control Panel

(Results vary from version to version)
Prank Quotient: High   *Security Quotient:* High

The Control Panel is something like the central workshop of the operating system where almost all settings and properties can be changed. It can be accessed via the Start menu by clicking on Start > Settings > Control Panel. Typically, one can find a number of different settings pages like *Sounds and Multimedia, Add/Remove Hardware, Date/Time* and many others. It is actually possible to almost completely change the look and feel of all settings pages.

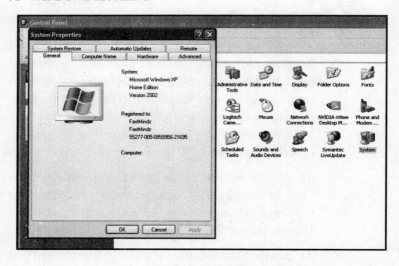

Each settings page in the Control Panel actually represents information stored in a particular .cpl file located in the system folder. In other words, the contents, looks and feel of each settings page is actually controlled by its corresponding .cpl file. For example, the Multimedia Properties settings page represents the *mmsys.cpl* file stored in the system folder. These .cpl files contain the key to changing the complete contents, look and feel by simply following the steps below:

1. Identify the Control Panel settings page (to be customized) and its respective .cpl file through either trial and error techniques or by simply referring to the table given here:

Control Panel Page	.CPL File
Add/Remove Programs	Appwiz.cpl
Display Properties	Desk.cpl
Regional Settings	Intl.cpl
Fax Settings	Fax.cpl
Hardware Wizard Settings	Hdwwiz.cpl
Internet Properties	Inetcpl.cpl

(Contd.)

Control Panel Page	.CPL File
Infrared Port Settings	Irprops.cpl
International/Regional	Intl.cpl
Mouse Properties	Main.cpl
Game Controllers	Joy.cpl
Multimedia Properties	Mmsys.cpl
Modem Settings	Modem.cpl
Network Settings	Netcpl.cpl
Ports Settings	Ports.cpl
Passwords	Password.cpl
Power Configuration	Powercfg.cpl
System Properties	Sysdm.cpl
Dialing Properties	Telephon.cpl
Scanners and Camera	Sticpl.cpl
Date/Time Settings	Timedate.cpl
Accessibility Settings	Access.cpl
Desktop Themes	Themes.cpl

2. Change the attributes of the .cpl file through the *Attrib* command such that editing the file contents are allowed.

3. Open the .cpl file in the MSDOS-Editor in the following manner:

    c:\>cd winnt

    c:\winnt>cd system32

    c:\winnt\system32>edit /70 abc.cpl

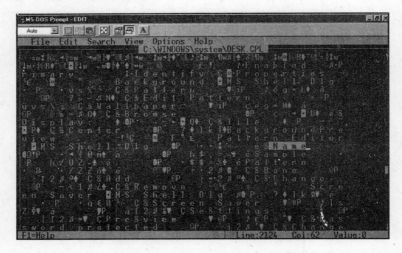

4. You are now in a position to change everything about the contents, look and feel of the respective Control Panel settings page.

5. Save the .cpl file and exit the MSDOS-Editor. The next time you open that particular Control Panel settings page you will be able to view the changes.

Hiding Control Panel Settings Pages

(For all Windows versions)

Prank Quotient: Medium   *Security Quotient:* High

It is possible to hide specific settings pages from within the Control Panel. Sometimes, such a feature cannot only be a great security feature, but can also restrict a user's movements to a great extent. This hidden Windows feature can be made active by simply following the steps below:

1. Open the *regedit.exe* file.

2. Search or scroll down to the following registry key:

   HKEY_CURRENT_USER\Control Panel\don't load

3. For each Control Panel settings page that you wish to hide, create a new string entry whose name is the same as the settings page's corresponding .cpl filename. Please refer to the table in the previous example for complete filename list.

4. Set the data value of the string entry to *No* to hide the control panel setting page, and to *Yes* to display it.

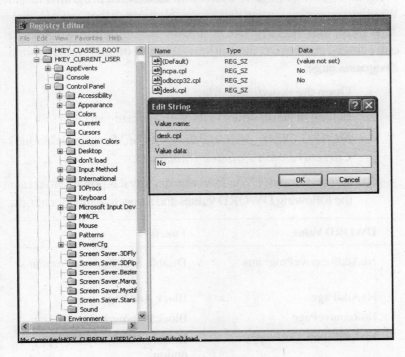

5. Exit the Windows registry. You might have to restart the Windows session for the changes to come into effect.

It is also possible to implement the above by simply creating and executing a file with a .reg extension containing the data given below:

REGEDIT4

[HKEY_CURRENT_USER\Control Panel\don't load]

"Complete .cpl filename"="No or Yes"

Customizing the Add/Remove Programs Page (Control Panel)

(For Windows 2000, XP and ME)

Prank Quotient: High   *Security Quotient:* High

As the name suggests, users usually use the *Add/Remove Programs* settings page to either add or remove programs to the Windows operating system. It is accessible through the Control Panel. This particular registry tweak allows system administrators to completely customize the various settings of this *Add/Remove Programs* page:

1. Open the *regedit.exe* file.

2. Search or scroll down to the following registry key:

    HKEY_LOCAL_MACHINE\Software\Microsoft\Windows\ CurrentVersion\Policies\Uninstall

3. Within the above Windows registry key it is possible to create the following DWORD values and respective functionalities:

DWORD Value	Function
NoAddRemovePrograms	Disable Add/Remove Programs
NoAddPage	Block Add Page.
NoRemovePage	Block Remove Page.
NoAddFromCDorFloppy	Disable Add from CD/Floppy option.
NoAddFromInternet	Disable Add from Internet option.
NoAddFromNetwork	Disable Add from Network option.
NoServices	Disable other services option.
NoWindowsSetupPage	Disable Windows Wizard.
NoSupportInfo	Hide Support Information.

It is important to note that in each of the above cases, setting the DWORD value to 1 enables the restriction, while setting it to 0 disables it.

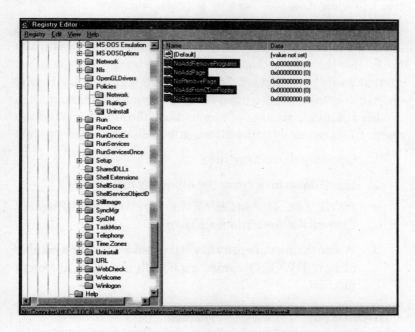

4. Exit the Windows registry. You might have to restart the Windows session for the changes to come into effect.

It is also possible to implement the above by simply creating and executing a file with a .reg extension containing the data below:

REGEDIT4

[HKEY_LOCAL_MACHINE\Software\Microsoft\Windows\ CurrentVersion\Policies\Uninstall]

"DWORD Value"="Data Value 0 or 1"

Blocking Automatic Start up of Programs

(For all Windows versions)

Prank Quotient: Low   *Security Quotient:* High

Most malicious programs like viruses, trojans, keyloggers and others are based upon the principle that they can be automatically loaded into the memory each time Windows boots. This automatic start can easily be configured through a simple registry entry. Hence, on many occasions it is a good idea for system administrators to disable automatic starting of applications through the Windows registry. This can easily be done through the following registry tweak:

1.   Open the *regedit.exe* file.

2.   Scroll down to or create the following registry key:

     HKEY_LOCAL_MACHINE\Software\Microsoft\Windows\ CurrentVersion\Policies\Explorer

3.   Within the above registry key, it is possible to create a number of new DWORD entries each with a slightly different function:

DWORD Entry	Function
DisableLocalMachineRun	Disables all applications from automatic start up during all sessions on that machine.
DisableLocalMachineRunOnce	Disables all applications from automatic start up during the next session on that machine.
DisableCurrentUserRun	Disables all applications from automatic start up during all sessions of the particular user.
DisableCurrentUserRunOnce	Disables all applications from automatic start up during the next session of the user.

It is important to note that in each case, a data value of 1 prevents applications from automatically running each time Windows loads, while a data value of 0 enables automatic running.

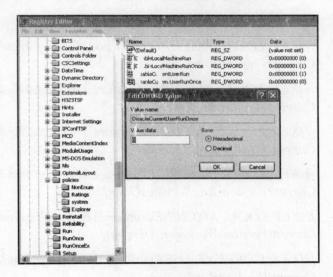

4. Exit the Windows registry. You might need to restart the Windows session for the changes to come into affect.

It is also possible to implement the above by simply creating and executing a .reg extension file containing the data as below:

REGEDIT4

[HKEY_LOCAL_MACHINE\Software\Microsoft\Windows\CurrentVersion\ Policies\Explorer]

"DWORD Entry" = "Value"

Preventing Specific Applications from Running Automatically

(For all Windows versions)

Prank Quotient: Low   *Security Quotient:* High

Taking the previous example a bit further it is actually possible to selectively prevent specific applications from being automatically loaded into the memory each time Windows boots. This can be carried out in the following manner:

1. Open the *regedit.exe* file.

2. Scroll down to the following registry keys:

    [HKEY_LOCAL_MACHINE\Software\Microsoft\Windows\ CurrentVersion\Run]

    [HKEY_LOCAL_MACHINE\Software\Microsoft\Windows\ CurrentVersion\RunOnce]

    [HKEY_LOCAL_MACHINE\Software\Microsoft\Windows\ CurrentVersion\RunServices]

    [HKEY_LOCAL_MACHINE\Software\Microsoft\Windows\ CurrentVersion\RunServicesOnce]

    [HKEY_LOCAL_MACHINE\Software\Microsoft\WindowsNT\ CurrentVersion\Winlogon\Userinit]

    [HKEY_CURRENT_USER\Software\Microsoft\Windows\ CurrentVersion\Run]

    [HKEY_CURRENT_USER\Software\Microsoft\Windows\ CurrentVersion\RunOnce]

    [HKEY_CURRENT_USER\Software\Microsoft\Windows\ CurrentVersion\RunServices]

    [HKEY_CURRENT_USER\Software\Microsoft\Windows\ CurrentVersion\RunServicesOnce]

    [HKEY_CURRENT_USER\Software\Microsoft\WindowsNT\ CurrentVersion\Windows]

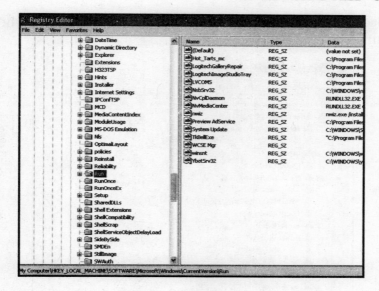

3. Within the above registry keys, look for and delete corresponding entries of the applications that you want to prevent from automatically getting loaded into the Windows registry.

4. Other places that one can also look are the Start Up folder (*C:\WINDOWS\Start Menu\Programs\StartUp*) and the *Win.ini* file.

5. Exit the Windows registry. You might need to restart the Windows session for the changes to come into effect.

Customizing the MSN Messenger Warning Message

(For all Windows versions)
Prank Quotient: Medium   *Security Quotient:* Medium

Each time one starts a new MSN Messenger chat session one is greeted by a warning message that goes something like the following:

Never give out your password or credit card number in an instant message conversation.

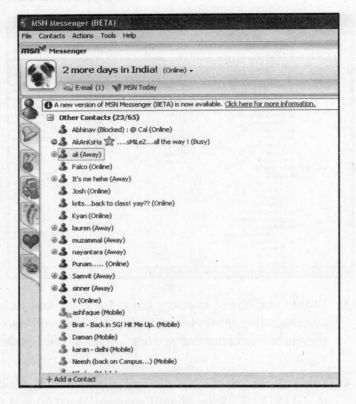

It is actually possible to replace this warning message with your own customized one with the help of a hidden windows registry tweak that can be executed in the following steps:

1. Open the regedit.exe file.

2. Scroll down to or create the following registry key:

   HKEY_LOCAL_MACHINE\SOFTWARE\Microsoft\ MessengerService\Policies

3. Create a new string value named *IMWarning* within the above registry key and set its data value to the customized welcome message that you want displayed each time a new MSN messenger chat session is started.

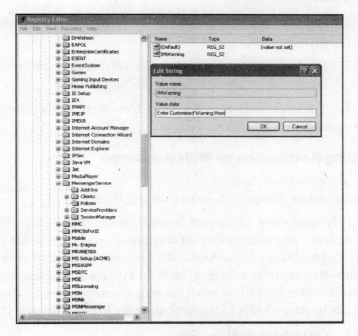

4. Exit the Windows registry. You might need to restart MSN Messenger for the changes to come into effect.

It is also possible to implement the above by simply creating and executing a .reg extension file containing the below data:

REGEDIT4

[HKEY_LOCAL_MACHINE\SOFTWARE\Microsoft\MessengerService \Policies]

"IMWarning"="Enter Customized Welcome Message"

Customizing the MSN Messenger Background Image

(For all Windows versions)
Prank Quotient: Medium   *Security Quotient:* Low

Newer versions of MSN Messenger allow users to customize the background image according to their personal preferences. Ever wondered how MSN Messenger does this? It is actually possible to replicate the same affect by simply following the steps below:

1. Go to the installation directory where MSN Messenger has been installed.

2. Replace the *lvback.gif* image file with the new customized image that you want to use as the background.

3. You might need to restart MSN Messenger for the changes to come into effect.

Putting Restrictions on MSN Messenger

(For all Windows versions)
Prank Quotient: Medium   *Security Quotient:* High

It is quite easy to look at Instant Messengers—like MSN Messenger—as a menace that not only poses a security risk but can also lead to privacy invasion attacks. Hence, a number of system administrators prefer to keep a check on a user's MSN Messenger activities. There are a few small but effective security restrictions that can be put on MSN Messenger using the Windows registry:

1. Open the *regedit.exe* file.

2. Scroll down to or create the following registry key:

    HKEY_LOCAL_MACHINE\Software\Policies\Microsoft\ Messenger\Client

3. Within the above registry key, it is possible to create a number of new DWORD values with the following names and functions:

DWORD Name	Restriction
DisableFileTransfer	Prevent File Transfer.
DisablePC2PCAudio	Prevent Audio Chat.
DisablePC2Phone	Prevent call to Phones.
DisableVideo	Prevent Video Chat.
PreventAutoUpdate	Prevent Auto MSN Update.
PreventBackgroundDownload	Self-Explanatory.
PreventConsumerVersion	Self-Explanatory.

4. In each case, one can set the DWORD value to 1 to enable the particular restriction, and to 0 to disable it.

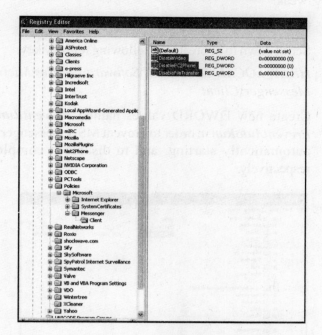

5. Exit the Windows registry. You might need to restart MSN Messenger for the change to come into effect.

It is also possible to implement the above by simply creating and executing a .reg extension file containing the undermentioned data:

REGEDIT4

[HKEY_LOCAL_MACHINE\Software\Policies\Microsoft\Messenger\Client]

"DWORD Name"="Value"

Disabling MSN Messenger

(For all Windows versions and up till MSN Messenger version 4x)

Prank Quotient: Medium   *Security Quotient:* High

On certain occasions it is best to completely disable the MSN Messenger service, which is possible with the help of the following registry tweak:

1. Open the *regedit.exe* file.

2. Scroll down to or create the following registry key:

    HKEY_LOCAL_MACHINE\Software\Policies\Microsoft\ Messenger\Client

3. Create new DWORD values named *PreventRun* and *PreventAutoRun* in order to prevent MSN messenger from automatically starting, and to disable it completely, respectively.

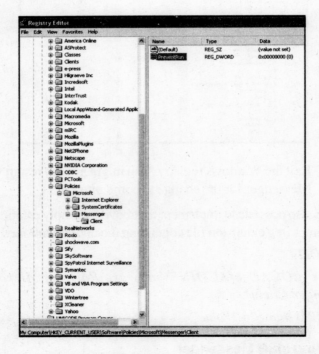

4. The above DWORD values can be set to 1 to enable the restriction, and to 0 to disable it.

5. Exit the Windows registry. You might need to restart MSN Messenger for the change to come into effect. Depending upon the restriction that you made, you may or may not be able to even start the Messenger!

It is also possible to implement the above by simply creating and executing a .reg extension file containing the undermentioned data:

REGEDIT4

[HKEY_LOCAL_MACHINE\Software\Policies\Microsoft\Messenger\Client]

"DWORD Name"="Value"

Simulating a Desktop Earthquake

(For all Windows versions)
Prank Quotient: High   *Security Quotient:* Low

The Windows operating system provides a number of unique opportunities to users to play a trick on an unsuspecting friend. One of the most popular tricks, or rather visual illusions, that some people play is called the *desktop earthquake* trick. This can easily be executed with the help of a simple JavaScript script as shown in the following code snippet:

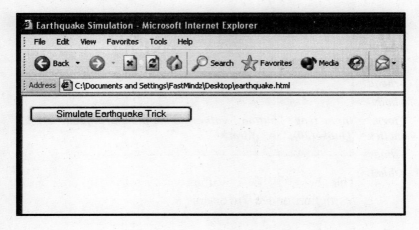

```
<?xml version="1.0" encoding="iso-8859-1"?>
<!DOCTYPE html PUBLIC "-//W3C//DTD XHTML 1.0 Transitional//EN"
"http://www.w3c.org/TR/xhtmll/DTD/xhtmll-transitional.dtd">
<html>
<head>
<title>Earthquake Simulation</title>
<script language="javaScript" type="text/javascript">
<!—
function Quake(time)
{
 if (self.moveBy)
 {
  for (var side = 25; side > 0; side=side-1)
  {
   for (var tmp = time; tmp > 0; tmp=tmp-1)
   {
      self.moveBy(0,side);
      self.moveBy(side,0);
      self.moveBy(0,-side);
      self.moveBy(-side,0);
   }
  }
 }
}
//—>
</script>
</head>
<body>
<form><input type="button" value="Simulate Earthquake Trick"
onclick="Quake(20);"/></form>
</body>
</html>
```

_____ SECURITY CHECKLISTS _____

1. Checklist for Choosing a Strong Password

✓ Your password should not be a word that appears in the dictionary (to prevent dictionary based attacks)

✓ Your password should not be *blank* or same as your username.

✓ Your password should be a combination of alphabets, numbers and special characters. Ideally, one should try and use both lowercase and uppercase characters.

✓ Your password should not be your name followed by your birth date. For example, one should not have a password like ankit2405.

✓ Your passwords should not be repeated.

✓ Your password MUST be changed regularly.

✓ Your password should not be written on a post-it note or a piece of paper stuck on your monitor or behind your CPU.

✓ You should not use the same password at multiple places.

✓ Your password should not be that random that even you forget it yourself!

2. Checklist for Securing a Home Computer (Basic)

✓ Run *Windows Update* at least once a week to patch your system against the latest vulnerabilities, loopholes and exploits.

✓ Use a strong password (Refer to earlier checklist).

✓ Install some good Antivirus software and update its virus definition files at least once a week to ward off the latest viruses, worms and trojans.

✓ Install a basic firewall (like Zonealarm, BlackIce or your favourite antivirus software's inbuilt firewall) on your system. This shall keep you notified of any live attacks, malicious data or probes.

✓ Try to connect to the Internet only after connecting to a proxy server.

✓ Install a Anti-spyware tool on your computer which will detect and remove any spyware tools on your computer.